DOG BREEDS

Siberian Huskies

by Anne Wendorff

Consultant:
Michael Leuthner, D.V.M.
PetCare Clinic, Madison, Wisc.

BLASTOFF!
4
READERS

BELLWETHER MEDIA · MINNEAPOLIS, MN

Note to Librarians, Teachers, and Parents:

Blastoff! Readers are carefully developed by literacy experts and combine standards-based content with developmentally appropriate text.

Level 1 provides the most support through repetition of high-frequency words, light text, predictable sentence patterns, and strong visual support.

Level 2 offers early readers a bit more challenge through varied simple sentences, increased text load, and less repetition of high-frequency words.

Level 3 advances early-fluent readers toward fluency through increased text and concept load, less reliance on visuals, longer sentences, and more literary language.

Level 4 builds reading stamina by providing more text per page, increased use of punctuation, greater variation in sentence patterns, and increasingly challenging vocabulary.

Level 5 encourages children to move from "learning to read" to "reading to learn" by providing even more text, varied writing styles, and less familiar topics.

Whichever book is right for your reader, Blastoff! Readers are the perfect books to build confidence and encourage a love of reading that will last a lifetime!

This edition first published in 2010 by Bellwether Media, Inc.

No part of this publication may be reproduced in whole or in part without written permission of the publisher. For information regarding permission, write to Bellwether Media, Inc., Attention: Permissions Department, 5357 Penn Avenue South, Minneapolis, MN 55419.

Library of Congress Cataloging-in-Publication Data
Wendorff, Anne.
 Siberian huskies / by Anne Wendorff.
   p. cm. — (Blastoff! Readers dog breeds)
 Includes bibliographical references and index.
 Summary: "Simple text and full-color photography introduce beginning readers to the characteristics of the dog breed Siberian huskies. Developed by literacy experts for students in kindergarten through third grade"—Provided by publisher.
 ISBN 978-1-60014-303-8 (hardcover : alk. paper)
 1. Siberian husky—Juvenile literature. I. Title.
 SF429.S65W46 2010
 636.73—dc22

                              2009037212

Printed in the United States of America, North Mankato.
010110   1149

Contents

What Are Siberian Huskies?   4

History of Siberian Huskies   8

Siberian Huskies Today   12

Glossary   22

To Learn More   23

Index   24

What Are Siberian Huskies?

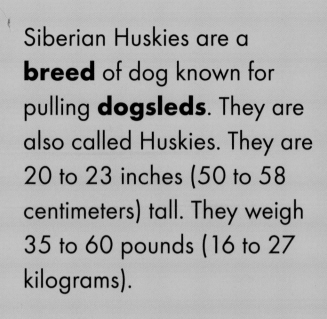

Siberian Huskies are a **breed** of dog known for pulling **dogsleds**. They are also called Huskies. They are 20 to 23 inches (50 to 58 centimeters) tall. They weigh 35 to 60 pounds (16 to 27 kilograms).

Huskies have blue or brown eyes. Some Huskies have one blue eye and one brown eye.

Huskies grow two layers of hair to keep warm. Their outer layer of hair is thick and straight. Their inner layer of hair is soft and fuzzy. Huskies **shed** their inner layer of hair twice a year.

Their hair is usually black, white, brown, or red. Their tails curve upward and are covered by thick hair.

fun fact

Huskies have color patterns called markings in the hair around their heads.

History of Siberian Huskies

Huskies are from northern Asia. They were bred to work in cold weather. Their job was to pull dogsleds across the snow. The dogsleds carried people, food, and supplies. Huskies are called **Arctic dogs** because they can work and live in cold weather.

Huskies came to Alaska in the early 1900s. They were used as **working dogs** to pull dogsleds during gold rushes. Huskies also helped rescue people lost in the snow.

fun fact

The U.S. Army used Huskies in search and rescue missions during World War II.

The **American Kennel Club (AKC)** decided Huskies were an official dog breed in 1930. They became members of the working group of dog breeds.

Siberian Huskies Today

Huskies compete against other working dogs at dog shows. Huskies are strong and smart.

This makes them good at tracking, **agility**, obedience, and strength events. Huskies often win events because they enjoy working hard.

Huskies also compete in dogsled races. The **Iditarod** is the biggest dogsled race in the world. Huskies pull dogsleds across 1,150 miles (1,850 kilometers) of snow! The temperature is below freezing during the race. Huskies pull their dogsleds across mountains and through forests. The dogsled that finishes first is the winner!

fun fact

Most dogsled races are more than 400 miles (643 kilometers) long.

Huskies are friendly and outgoing dogs. They are kind and gentle. They are also known to howl rather than bark. This makes them bad **guard dogs**.

Huskies enjoy living with other dogs or people. They do not like to be left alone.

Huskies do many different jobs. They are often trained to be **therapy dogs**. Therapy dogs help make people happy. Huskies make good therapy dogs because they are very friendly.

Huskies are still used to pull dogsleds and work in cold weather.

Today, most Huskies are **companion dogs**. Companion dogs live with people as pets. Huskies are good companion dogs because they are playful and loyal!

Glossary

agility—a dog sport where dogs run through a series of obstacles

American Kennel Club (AKC)—a group that monitors and promotes purebred dogs

Arctic dogs—dogs from the cold area around the Arctic Circle

breed—a type of dog

companion dogs—dogs that provide friendship to people

dogsled—a sled that some dog breeds pull across snow

guard dog—a dog that barks or alerts its owner when strangers are near

Iditarod—the longest dogsled race in the world

shed—to lose hair

therapy dogs—dogs that provide comfort to people

working dogs—dogs that do jobs to help people; Huskies were bred to pull sleds in cold weather.

To Learn More

AT THE LIBRARY

Blake, Robert J. *Togo*. New York, N.Y.: Philomel Books, 2002.

Hengel, Katherine. *Strong Siberian Huskies*. Edina, Minn.: ABDO Publishing, 2009.

London, Jonathan. *Sled Dogs Run*. New York, N.Y.: Walker & Co., 2005.

ON THE WEB

Learning more about Siberian Huskies is as easy as 1, 2, 3.

1. Go to www.factsurfer.com.

2. Enter "Siberian Huskies" into the search box.

3. Click the "Surf" button and you will see a list of related Web sites.

With factsurfer.com, finding more information is just a click away.

Index

1900s, 10
1930, 11
agility, 13
Alaska, 10
American Kennel Club (AKC), 11
Arctic dogs, 9
Asia, 9
breed, 5, 11
cold weather, 9, 19
companion dogs, 20
dog shows, 12
dogsled racing, 14, 15
dogsleds, 5, 9, 10, 14, 19
eyes, 5
gold rushes, 10
guard dogs, 16
hair, 6, 7
height, 5
howling, 16

Iditarod, 14
markings, 7
obedience events, 13
rescue, 10
shedding, 6
strength events, 13
therapy dogs, 18
tracking, 13
weight, 5
working dogs, 10, 11, 12
World War II, 10